JESUS — A PORTRAIT OF LOVE

JESUS — A PORTRAIT OF LOVE

A Meditation on Matthias Gruenewald's Isenheim Altar

M. Martyria Madauss

Evangelical Sisterhood of Mary
Darmstadt, West Germany

JESUS — A PORTRAIT OF LOVE, revised edition 1977
© Evangelical Sisterhood of Mary, 1972
ISBN 3 87209 603 6

Original Title: JESUS VOR AUGEN GEMALT
First German Edition — 1972
First English Edition — 1972
Translated into Dutch, Finnish, French, Italian and Norwegian

Unless otherwise stated, all Bible quotations are taken from the Revised Standard Version of the Bible, copyrighted 1946 and 1952 by the Division of Christian Education of the National Council of the Churches of Christ in the U.S.A., and used by permission.

The reproductions of the pictures of Matthias Gruenewald's Isenheim Altar are mainly from colour slides taken by the Evangelical Sisterhood of Mary at the Musée d'Unterlinden, Colmar, France — the present location of the altar — by kind permission of the Société Schongauer.

The background of the Gothic, chapel-like room, in which the altar now stands, was included in some of the photographs in order to give an impression of its present setting.

Printed in West Germany

JESUS — A PORTRAIT OF LOVE

The Isenheim Altar by Matthias Gruenewald is one of the most outstanding works of art of all times. It is a unique presentation of the Gospel message: We are not lost in our sin; we have been saved by Jesus Christ, and our names are written in heaven. Gruenewald depicted these glad tidings in such a way that we cannot but love Jesus when we contemplate his paintings.

To love Jesus truly and sincerely — this was my heart's desire even as a young girl. However, this "first love" faded away. Another great love gained an ever-increasing hold over my heart. It was the love of art. The time that I should have spent with Jesus in prayer and meditation on His Word I devoted to art instead. Consequently, this "first love" departed from me, without my realizing it.

But what did our Lord Jesus Christ do? On my way to Paris to visit the Louvre, He led me to Colmar, where, purely because of my interest in the history of art, I wished to see Gruenewald's Isenheim Altar. However, this portrait of love showed me Jesus more vividly than I had ever seen Him before. I was granted deep repentance as I realized that Jesus no longer had first priority in my heart, but that I had allowed art to take that place. From this point on, the Lord directed the course of my life in such a way that I was time and again confronted with that searching question of His, "Do you love Me?" Thus my "first love", which had grown cold, was renewed and deepened by the grace of His forgiveness.

For me it was a seal of Jesus' forgiveness that He later created in me the longing to proclaim Him in His great love for us men, as He is depicted for us in the paintings of Matthias Gruenewald. If the Lord would use the following pages with Gruenewald's paintings to show how much Jesus loves us and has suffered for our sake, I would consider it a sign of His great grace.

Have this mind among
yourselves, which you have in
CHRIST JESUS,
who, though he was in the form
of God, did not count equality
with God a thing to be grasped,
but emptied himself,
taking the form of a servant,
being born in the likeness of men.
And being found in human form
he humbled himself
and became obedient unto death
even death on a cross.

Therefore God has highly
exalted him and bestowed on him
the name which is above
every name,
that at the name of Jesus
every knee should bow,
in heaven and on earth, and
under the earth,
and every tongue confess
that Jesus Christ is Lord,
to the glory of God the Father.

Phil. 2

GRUENEWALD — IN YOUTH AND OLD AGE

A portrait of Master Gruenewald in his youth. His real name may have been Mathis Gothardt Neidhardt, but we cannot be sure. Only little is known about his life. Like Leonardo da Vinci, he is reputed to have had great scientific knowledge, especially in designing fountains. Indeed, he must have been a universal genius. For a long time scholars have tried to discover more about Master Gruenewald, but to no avail. Gruenewald evidently wished to remain silent about his life. His sole desire was to proclaim Jesus Christ and Him alone, in accordance with the words of John the Baptist, "He must increase, but I must decrease." Thus not only did Gruenewald preach through his paintings, but his paintings were backed by the testimony of his life, since he chose obscurity for Jesus' sake. However, the greatest things are often born out of obscurity.

It was in obscurity that Gruenewald portrayed the greatest mystery that the world has ever known: Jesus Christ was born for us, and for our sake He suffered, died and rose from the dead.

Gruenewald is said to have been born about 1460 in Wuerzburg, Germany. For a long time he lived in Aschaffenburg, but he also worked in Alsace-Lorraine for a while.

If we compare the youth portrait with **Gruenewald's self-portrait as an old man**, we can discern the great change that took place in his life. In the first picture a young man, filled with expectation, looks out into the world. In the second picture it is evident from the rapt expression on the face of the old man that he is enthralled by Jesus alone.

According to the few historical facts known, Gruenewald was gripped by the spirit of the Reformation. In his heart burned the Good News: "justified by faith in Jesus Christ alone!" It is said that after his death at Halle in 1528 some of Luther's writings were found among his possessions.

PLATES 1 a + 1 b

ANTHONY ENTHRONED

When Gruenewald went to Isenheim, he came into contact with a monastery of the order of St. Anthony, where the monks cared for lepers and victims of the plague. A large carved shrine of St. Anthony, the patron saint of the monastery, had been set up there. Anthony is seated on a throne in the centre of the shrine. On the right stands Jerome, the scholar, whose symbol is the lion. On the left, Augustine, the church father, with crook in hand.

Carved wooden shrines like this were customary in those days and were regarded as very valuable. When the Abbot of Isenheim had this shrine erected, he was prompted by love for the patients who were being cared for in his hospital. Since the wooden shrine was highly valuable, it was to be enclosed by paintings during the week. Accordingly, the artist Gruenewald was summoned and commissioned to make an altar with movable panels that would adorn the precious wooden shrine with side pictures and cover it with a double layer of pictures. Both the front and back of each pair of wings could be used by Gruenewald as canvases for his pictures.

When the wings were open, they formed a frame for the shrine. Gruenewald used these two innermost sides for his portrayals of Anthony. On the left Anthony is shown in conversation with the hermit Paul, one of his contemporaries, and on the right he is shown in temptation.

The Abbot of Isenheim, who wished to magnify Anthony's greatness by erecting a shrine in his honour, now had to watch Gruenewald do the exact opposite in his portrayals. For Gruenewald knew that when man is enthroned, death reigns, because everything that is human will be devoured by moths and rust. Only when the Lord is on the throne, can eternal, divine life triumph.

PLATES 2 a + 2 b

The side paintings of the carved wooden shrine:
ANTHONY SPEAKING WITH PAUL, THE HERMIT

What does Gruenewald want to say with this picture? Looking at the carved figures (plate 2), we see that St. Anthony is sitting on his throne like a king, proudly erect, sure of himself and arrogant. His very bearing is expressive of the thought, "What more do I need?" But in the painting he is shown in a completely different situation. He is portrayed as someone in real need of advice. Gruenewald seems to depict the hermit as saying to Anthony, "If you are a great man, a shepherd of the flock, if you have a high position, beware of domineering instead of serving — for if you domineer, you will bring forth no fruit!"

It is evident that this is the message that Paul is trying to impress upon St. Anthony, for although Paul is humbly dressed in a braided garment, expressive of his poverty, above him is a palm tree in blossom — the symbol of fertility. A raven brings him bread and at his feet lies a tame doe. Paul's outward appearance is in sharp contrast to that of the luxuriously clad Anthony seated before withered trees and a barren rock. With all his being Paul is preaching to Anthony that it is of utmost importance to follow Jesus' example of true poverty and go the way of complete self-denial. Only then will the fruits of grace grow (Psalm 1:3) — but never if we put on a "cloak of piety". This is indicated by the contrast between Anthony's blue cloak and Paul's earth-coloured garment.

With his hand Paul makes an emphatic gesture, as if to implore us, "Abandon your high and arrogant ways. Follow Jesus' way, the way of lowliness." We are reminded of the words of the Apostle Paul to the Church at Philippi, "Let this mind be in you, which was also in Christ Jesus" (Philippians 2:5 AV). He humbled Himself. Only if we walk the way of lowliness with Jesus, will our life be fruitful. The more proud and domineering we are, the less fruit we shall bear. The more unassuming we are — perhaps even laughed at and ridiculed by others for Jesus Christ's sake — the more fruit we shall bring for eternity. Gruenewald has a special message to proclaim here: wealth and honour are harmful to Christianity. The Church of Jesus Christ can have true life only if she shares the poverty of her Lord.

PLATE 3

The representation of **Paul** reminds us of the self-portrait that Gruenewald sketched in his old age — the same eyes beholding divine mysteries that can be seen only when we are united with Jesus in love.

It is worth giving up everything for Jesus, for the things of this world give us no lasting happiness, but only sorrow. They bring ever increasing distress upon us. Jesus, however, grants us a glimpse of heaven and the eternal glory even here on earth — in Himself.

To return to **Anthony**. Before he found Jesus, he lived like a "rich, young ruler" in Cairo, a large and permissive city. He then entered the solitude of the desert in order to live exclusively for Jesus. And there he experienced the truth of what Luther said, "We are beggars up to our last moment on earth." The picture of Anthony in temptation (on the other side of the carved shrine — see plate 5) demonstrates this truth and reminds us that we cannot master our sin by ourselves. We can only entreat Jesus Christ to renew and change us by the power of His redemption.

PLATES 4 a + 4 b

What a contrast to the carving of Anthony sitting on the throne! Here Master Gruenewald proclaims the truth of Holy Scripture: man in all his glory is dethroned, a mere nothing because of his sin — unless he has become a new creation in Christ, our Saviour. As the enemy and adversary of our Lord Jesus Christ, Satan rages against the believers. But Jesus, in His great love, uses these attacks to unmask us, so that when we feel at times as though we are at the mercy of the powers of darkness, we shall cry out for Him all the more, like Anthony in this picture. The small piece of white parchment in the lower right hand corner of the picture bears Anthony's desperate cry, "Where were You, dear Jesus, where were You? Why weren't You there to heal my wounds?" Anthony, in utter weakness, feels as though he is delivered up to the powers of darkness, who are trying to take away his faith in Jesus' victory.

Here Gruenewald shows that he is not an idealist but rather a realist, who stands on the solid ground of Holy Scripture. Satan and his demons are a reality in our lives, whether we want to believe it or not. The Word of God tells us this with unmistakable clarity. God permits Satan to tempt us, so that we shall come to realize how weak and sinful we are, tempted by our thirst for recognition, demand for attention, our spirit of criticism and carnal desires. Usually it is not until we undergo severe temptations that we realize how very much we need the grace of Jesus' redemption.

The more the temptations make us aware of our utter helplessness, the more we begin to yearn for Jesus and Him alone and to cling to Him with all our being. We must go through the sufferings of these temptations, as Anthony did, to learn to weep over our sins and then to drink of the grace of Jesus like a person dying of thirst.

Despite appearances, however, Anthony is not at the mercy of the powers of hell. For above this horrible scene the heavens open and Jesus appears with the sign of victory — an experience which is not reserved exclusively for Anthony. It should be ours too. When we have to undergo temptation, we can have the comforting assurance that the greater the temptation, the closer Jesus, the Victor, actually is to us, even if we cannot sense anything. Ultimately, the devil can achieve nothing, for at Calvary our Lord Jesus Christ has destroyed Satan's power. Jesus is Victor!

PLATE 5

When the first pair of wings, showing Anthony in conversation with Paul, and Anthony in temptation, are closed, four new pictures appear next to each other. From left to right these are: the annunciation, the angel concert, Mary with the Child Jesus, and the resurrection.

PLATE 6

THE ANNUNCIATION OF JESUS' BIRTH

Mary is kneeling at a chest in front of a red curtain — probably an indication that the angel's visit to Mary occurred in the midst of her everyday life and was totally unexpected.

"Behold, a virgin shall conceive, and bear a son, and shall call his name Immanuel" (Isaiah 7:14 AV). This tremendous promise — a prophecy made 700 years previously by Isaiah — now begins to be fulfilled with the angel's annunciation. Directly above Mary, in front of the window on the left, is a dove, the symbol of the Holy Spirit, who overshadows Mary, so that the Son of God may be born in her. Thus Mary becomes the temple of God. Gruenewald places a threefold seal upon this mystery. At the upper left is the Prophet Isaiah, who proclaims the promise; the Bible in front of Mary is opened at this very verse in Isaiah, and the angel's pointing hand emphasizes this message. The Holy Spirit sheds light on this amazing message and confirms it.

PLATE 7

Mary's hands are held out like an open vessel — open, in faith and trust, as she receives the will of God. They express her commitment, "Be it unto me according to thy word" (Luke 1:38 AV).

The hand of the Angel Gabriel, with its pointing gesture, pronounces her high calling and declares that that which God says is yea and amen: "Thou shalt ... bring forth a son, and shalt call his name JESUS" (Luke 1:31 AV).

The two pairs of hands, so different in appearance, are making the same eloquent proclamation. Mary's receptive hands, expressive of faith, and the pointing hand of the angel declare, "The Lord's will shall come to pass." The angel, with divine authority, delivers the greatest message since the words of creation were spoken. The Son of God will actually take on human form within Mary. And He will bring about a new creation — the new man.

PLATE 8

THE ANGELS REJOICE: GOD BECOMES MAN

"The Word was God ... and the Word became flesh and dwelt among us" (John 1:1, 14). The heavenly world rejoicing at the breath-taking miracle — this is the picture Gruenewald paints for us in his **angel concert**. Every song of the angels is in honour of Christ, the Desire of all the heavenly hosts and all the spirits and angels. Christ has come! The angels sing praises, because the proclamation of the Old Covenant has come to fulfilment. The promise given to the fathers has now been fulfilled. Salvation is being wrought!

It is clear that the Old Covenant is being depicted here. In the relief on the canopy above Mary we see Melchizedek pronouncing his blessing. In addition, we can see the design of fig leaves (the fig tree being the symbol of Israel) as well as prophets whose figures adorn the pillars. All who belong to the Old Covenant are rejoicing that at long last salvation is dawning.

Not only angels, but also mysterious beings are rejoicing — spirits with a strange aura about them, whom Gruenewald had perhaps seen in a vision. In this picture Gruenewald wants to say that salvation in Jesus Christ, which was proclaimed to Mary, will bring immeasurable joy to those of the Old Covenant too, who had struggled on in servitude to the Law.

The angels are amazed, astonished that the One whom they worship in heaven and whose glory they can never extol enough has become Man. Beside the Mother Mary is a bathtub. Gruenewald has added this very human touch in order to emphasize the reality of the incarnation of the Son of God.

The whole angel concert is a resounding anthem of praise about the redemption. Redemption, which brings deliverance from our pride — we think of Anthony — from our helplessness and from our fruitlessness. The heavens resound with exultant praise, because salvation has been granted in Jesus.

PLATE 9

THE PROMISE IS FULFILLED

Mary is stepping over the threshold from the Old to the New Covenant. She has already been crowned for her faith. There is something unreal and yet very real about the way Mary steps forward so that the eternal promise can be fulfilled.

> *My soul magnifies the Lord,*
> *and my spirit rejoices in God my Saviour,*
> *for he has regarded the low estate*
> *of his handmaiden.*
> *For behold, henceforth all generations*
> *will call me blessed.*
> *My soul magnifies the Lord,*
> *and my spirit rejoices in God my Saviour.*

Luke 1:46 ff.

Folded in prayer, her hands point to Christ, whom the heavenly hosts around her praise in joyful adoration. Her hands are still like those of a pure, young maiden. How different they will be beneath the cross when, marked with agony, they speak of quiet submission!

PLATE 10

CHRIST IS BORN

"A virgin shall conceive, and bear a son, and shall call his name Immanuel!" (Isaiah 7:14 AV). This event has come to pass! Christ was born at night, but Gruenewald turns the night into bright daylight. The night has been driven away. The sun is shining above Mary and the Child. Radiant light falls upon the divine Child in His loveliness. At the same time, however, He is shown in His full humanity with swaddling clothes and a little bed. Mary gazes upon the Child not only with the tenderness of a mother, but with the love of a bride as she beholds the long-awaited Messiah and Lord.

This painting illustrates the fact that Jesus can captivate a human heart so completely that we testify, "I saw no one but Jesus alone." To be satisfied by Him alone — this is the secret of Christianity and its source of life.

PLATE 11

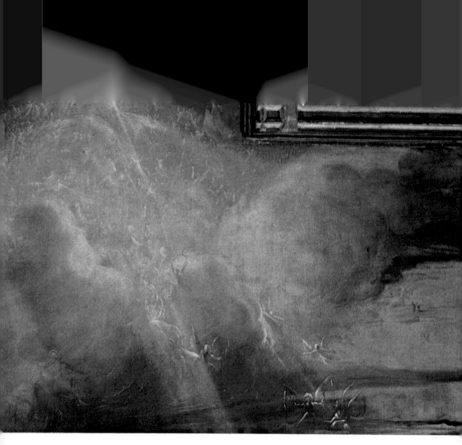

PLATE 12

In the open heavens above the Child Jesus and His mother, God the Father can be seen holding an orb and a sceptre and with Him are many angelic beings. All heaven is astir. By the love of God manifested in Jesus, the enemy has been put to flight and heaven is victorious.

At the birth of Jesus victory has already begun, for this heavenly Child will follow the path that no one else can tread. Pure and sinless, He will take away the sin of the world by treading the path of suffering. Mary is holding not only a little child in her arms, but the Saviour, whom John the Baptist will later refer to as the Bridegroom, saying he "rejoices greatly at the bridegroom's voice".

Not one of us can see Jesus aright unless he beholds Him with the love that says, "You alone are worthy of my love. I want to live my whole life for You alone and give You everything I have. This I will do."

PLATE 13

IF I ONLY HAVE YOU ...

To the right of Mary and the Child a church has been painted in the background to represent the Church of Jesus Christ on earth, and in front of it a rose — the rose being the symbol of love, the "first love" for Jesus. Gruenewald wants to say that Christians can only have true fellowship with Jesus if they truly love Him. The rose of bridal love for Jesus can only blossom in the Church if we can say, "If only I have You, there is nothing in heaven or on earth that I will desire!" The Christian life becomes tiresome, boring, yes, even repulsive when this rose no longer blossoms in our hearts. Only the fragrance of this love will draw others to Jesus.

PLATE 14

ONLY THROUGH THE CROSS!

To the left of Mary and the Child a cross is depicted in an arched doorway. Why? Because true fellowship of love with Jesus — as we see with Mary — can only be entered into by those who go through the cross. Only along this way do we find the fullness of joy and an open heaven. Jesus said to all who wish to belong to Him, "No one comes to the Father but by me." By Me, the crucified Lord!

PLATE 15

PLATE 16

JESUS' LOVE AND SUFFERING FOR OUR SAKE

When the altar wings with the paintings of the annunciation and the resurrection (plate 6) are closed, the picture of the crucifixion can be seen in the centre. No doubt this painting was shown above all during Holy Week.

For Gruenewald this picture was the most important one. His chief concern was to paint Jesus Christ in His divine love and suffering in order that people laden with sin could receive healing and comfort from the true source of life, our Saviour. Throughout the world people seeking salvation and redemption are drawn to the cross of Jesus, where our sins were put to death with Him.

The fact that John the Baptist is standing beneath the cross takes this picture out of its historical context, since he was no longer alive at the time of the crucifixion. His presence emphasizes the timelessness of the event — eternal salvation was wrought for the whole world.

Everyone who has suffered the temptations of Anthony now accepts the grace bestowed by Jesus and can say in adoration, "Behold, the Lamb of God, who takes away the sin of the world!" As soon as Jesus in His incomprehensible love and suffering for our sake has a large place in our hearts, our lives are filled with joy. But as soon as this space for Jesus decreases, our joy decreases too. Here the words of John the Baptist written above his outstretched hand hold true, "He must increase, but I must decrease."

While I was young, I discovered how important it is to "decrease" if we want to have true joy. In those days I underwent periods of sadness — sadness that comes upon us without any evident reason. At such times everything seems meaningless and we cannot be really happy. Although we can study what we please, although we may have a happy home or marriage, and even know Jesus and be following Him, such periods of sadness repeatedly come upon us.

Such sadness, however, stems from the fact that Jesus and the suffering He endured for us do not have a large enough place in our lives. We do not love Him enough for forgiving our sins and setting us free from them. Personally, I can testify that the more Jesus became the centre and essence of my life, the more these powers of sadness yielded. I became happy and was at peace even in the midst of trials and temptations.

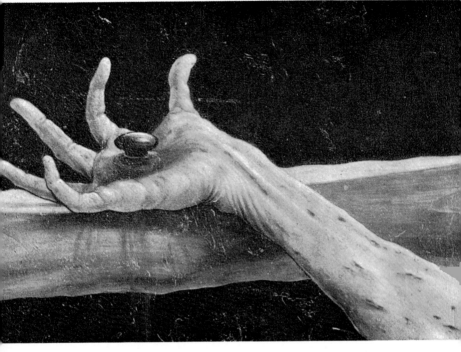

PLATE 17

An old tradition says that the beams of the cross were bent because the distance between the nail holes was too great for the hands and feet of our Lord Jesus to reach them; His limbs were torn out of joint. How this must have increased the pain and agony of our Lord, who sacrificed Himself for us! Jesus' pierced hands cry out to heaven for us, entreating the Father not to punish us according to our sins, but to grant us mercy and forgiveness for His sake.

JESUS MADE SIN FOR OUR SAKE

Gruenewald's concern was to show Jesus in His utter disfigurement as He hung upon the cross. In Isaiah 53 it is written that men hid their faces from Him. Why is this said of Christ? The reason is that He bore our abhorrent sins in His body on the tree, where He was put to death (1 Peter 2:24). All our pride, all our envy and desire for recognition, all our faultfinding and rebellion, yes, all our sins were put to death in Jesus Christ. We, who are sinners, are crucified with Christ and therefore raised with Him to walk in newness of life! (cf. Romans 6) In view of this truth we cannot be appalled enough at our sin.

Gruenewald — even if only in a very mild way — is a forerunner of the school of expressionist painting that emerged at the turn of the century. His representation of the body of Jesus appears to be naturalistic. Yet his main objective in creating this work of art is to portray the mystery: Christ crucified for the sake of our sin. Gruenewald accordingly depicted our sins on the body of the crucified Lord. The cruel eyes of the "unmerciful servant" (Matthew 18) seem to peer at us from the dark-coloured areas around the armpit to remind us of the sin of criticizing our neighbour. A little below this armpit of Jesus, it is possible to distinguish the tightly pressed lips of an accuser. Gruenewald also uses the loincloth as a means to depict sin. On the left, where the cloth is tied, he has painted two arrogant eyes. But only those who look beyond the naturalistic can see these things.

PLATE 18

JESUS' PIERCED FEET

When Gruenewald painted Jesus in His sufferings, he made Jesus' pierced feet almost resemble the form of an animal. In doing so, Gruenewald once again demonstrated that Jesus literally became sin in order to ransom us. Contemplating this portrayal of our crucified Lord, we realize that despair is the most serious sin of all. If we want to flee in despair as soon as we are confronted with our own evil, sinful image, thinking that we shall never change, we are saying that Jesus' suffering was in vain. Nothing grieves Jesus more than when we fall into the darkness of despair at the sight of our sin.

This we must never do — for Jesus' sake! He suffered immeasurably to procure our salvation. Therefore, when we do not trust Jesus to redeem us from every single sin, we commit the greatest sin that our sinful heart is capable of. Jesus let Himself be nailed to the cross, so that we need not remain in bondage to sin. If we have faith and abide in Him, He will set us free bit by bit. For He ransomed us by His suffering at Calvary. The temptations and chastenings we have to suffer because of our sin are nothing in comparison with the agony that Jesus endured on our behalf to blot out our sin.

When we see what Jesus has suffered for us, we can only be filled with the assurance, "My sins are forgiven. I have been set free to live a new life in Jesus Christ."

> *Thy wounded feet, dear Saviour,*
> *I yearn to clasp and hold.*
> *Look on me, Lord, with favour*
> *And from Thy cross behold*
> *My folded hands entreating*
> *That Thou wouldst say to me,*
> *"Let sorrow flee for ever!*
> *I have forgiven thee."*

PAUL GERHARDT

PLATE 19

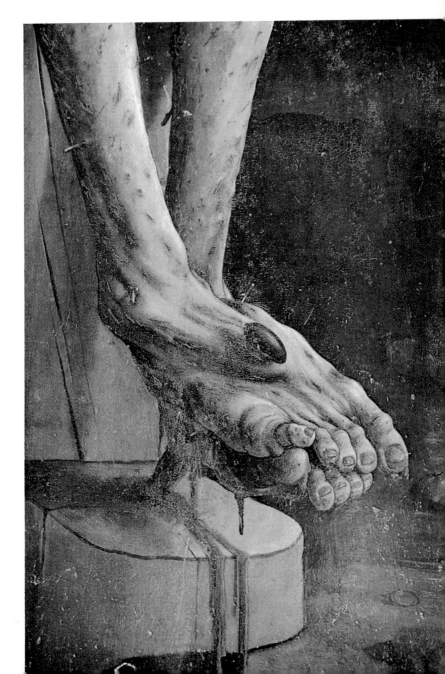

HERE WILL I STAND BESIDE THEE

John and the Mother Mary are standing beneath the cross. Here too Gruenewald did not paint naturalistic figures. He wanted to express the love for Jesus Christ that was in his own heart. For this reason the arm that John has placed around Mary is longer than it actually could be. This emphasizes the fact that John acted according to Jesus' words, "Behold your mother! Behold your son!" In Jesus Christ and beneath His cross we are one in love.

Mary's hands express her utter anguish at that which Jesus is enduring for us. Mary and John are suffering with Jesus in untold grief, because they love Him.

Today there is much cause for us to suffer with Jesus, since He is subjected to so much mockery and derision. Blasphemous musical productions are being presented in theatres and even churches. This ought to grieve us so much that we stand at Jesus' side all the more today — even if it entails suffering. The more we bring our sins to the cross in genuine contrition, the more we are constrained to endure ridicule and laughter for His sake, out of love for Him.

John and Mary are much larger proportionately than **Mary Magdalene**. From this we can perceive that the repentant cry, "Lord, forgive me my sins for the sake of Your blood", is surpassed by the fact that we then come to love Jesus with all our heart. And if we love Him, we want to stand by Him whenever He is mocked. This begins with the very small things in everyday life, for instance, by not conforming to the crowd.

PLATE 20

THOSE WHO ARE FORGIVEN MUCH LOVE MUCH
Luke 7

When Gruenewald painted Mary Magdalene beneath the cross, he again intentionally used the outward appearance to convey the spiritual meaning. The dark-coloured hem of her garment resembles a fleeing serpent. With this Gruenewald wants to say that beneath the cross of Jesus, when we are only able to cry out for mercy, all that is serpentlike and satanic, all that is sinful, will flee from us.

Every fibre in Mary Magdalene seems to be pleading, "Lord, forgive me! Lord, have mercy!" How wonderful it is that we can come to Jesus with this prayer every day, that He hears our pleas and has mercy upon us! This makes all the anguish of sin fade away! Her hands, which plead for mercy, will find their prayer answered. When we earnestly entreat Jesus, He will grant us release, deliverance from sin and an entirely new life, just as Mary Magdalene experienced. Thus with her whole being she also expresses her gratitude, "I thank You that You have taken away my sin!" The jar of ointment beside her signifies how lavish this thanks and love for Him must be.

PLATE 21

BEHOLD, THE LAMB OF GOD

To the right of the cross is **John the Baptist,** his appearance coarse and rugged as befitting his message of repentance. Yet with his tender, loving heart he was the first to recognize Jesus as "the Lamb of God, who takes away the sin of the world!" John the Baptist was enthralled by the Lamb of God. Gruenewald expresses this in the outstretched finger pointing to the crucified Lord and in John's words, "He must increase, but I must decrease!" Why are they words of supreme joy? As previously mentioned, the more we decrease, the more lowly and insignificant we become in our own eyes and in the sight of others, the more we confront and admit our sins, the more room Jesus will gain in us and the greater our joy will be in Him.

Jesus does not look to the right to Mary and John. His eyes are directed towards John the Baptist. It is as though the Lord is saying to John, who prepared the way for Him, "Was it not necessary that the Christ should suffer these things and enter into his glory?" And John seems to reply, "Yes, You are the Lamb of God, who takes away the sin of the world." The open Bible in the Baptist's hands indicates that which Gruenewald expresses: the death on the cross was in fulfilment of prophecy; God's eternal plans of salvation, proclaimed even on the very first pages of the Bible, have been fulfilled.

PLATE 22

O SACRED HEAD SORE WOUNDED ...

What great emphasis Gruenewald places on the thorns of Jesus!
For the sake of our sin Jesus had to bear the crown of thorns.
Satan was able to inflict this deepest of humiliations upon Jesus
because of our pride. If we are observant, we shall notice that
the representation of the crown of thorns is not naturalistic.
Above the ear of Jesus the crown of thorns is arched more than
one would expect. In this way Gruenewald expressed Satan's
burning hatred of Jesus. The dark holes to the left and right of
His ear seem to peer at us like two wicked eyes gloating over
the crucified Lord in the agony of His death.

The crown of thorns is above all a sign of disgrace. Whoever
wants to walk with Jesus, in true dedication, must be prepared
to bear disgrace. Such disgrace, however, will lead to a deeper
fellowship of love with Jesus.

PLATE 23

JESUS' BURIAL

Let us turn to a portion of the **predella** below the altar portraying Jesus' burial. John, the favourite disciple of Jesus, is holding his dead Lord in his arms. To the left is the Mother Mary in deep anguish.

We must all experience Jesus' burial in our lives. While Jesus hung on the cross and spoke, the disciples could still hope that He would suddenly descend from the cross. A miracle could have happened, for was He not the Son of God? But now at the burial, it was all over. The radiance of Jesus had vanished. And in their arms they were holding their dead Lord.

Whether young or old, we must all go through a similar experience in spirit. Jesus has drawn close to us. He has looked upon us. We have sensed His loving presence. And we have said to Him, "I desire You alone, nothing else." But then we have to undergo trials and temptations, and it seems to us as though Jesus were dead. He does not speak to us. He is silent. When we pray, we do not hear any answer. Nothing is more difficult in our lives than such a burial experience when we seem to be holding a dead Lord Jesus in our arms. But it is vital that we remain faithful in the night, when not a single star is shining, and believe: Jesus is risen! He is alive! He is Victor!

PLATE 24

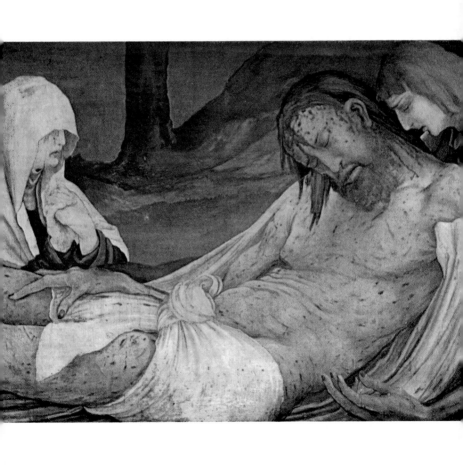

When the painting of the crucifixion is opened down the centre, the pictures of plate 6 reappear. On the far right we see Jesus' triumphant resurrection. The whole picture is wonderfully radiant with glowing colours and brilliant light, which sharply contrast with the night sky. In the glory of the resurrection, even the night is filled with stars and the joyous radiance of the angel concert is far surpassed by the fullness of joy expressed here.

Whereas in the crucifixion picture the body of Jesus is terribly disfigured, here His wonderful resurrection body can be seen. We are given a glimpse of the great Sun, Jesus, the Victor. All traces of maltreatment have disappeared. The wounds are now radiant, especially the one in His side. Suffering brings eternal glory and wounds are a majestic sign of victory. Gruenewald may deliberately have shown Jesus' garment pushed back on one side so as to reveal the glory of the wound in His heart.

Jesus raises His hands to impart His blessing in the power and authority of His resurrection. This He does daily for us and in doing so He majestically breaks asunder the chains binding us. If we endure in faith during the night of darkness when Jesus seems to be silent, if we are prepared to bear thorns with Jesus, that is, to suffer disgrace, to bear laughter and ridicule for His sake, He will live in us and His comfort will shine upon us like the warm rays of the sun. This is what the martyrs experienced when they suffered all manner of torture for Jesus' sake. Jesus lived in them to such an extent that He was greater than all the pain and anguish.

In eternity we shall have to stand before the glorified Lord and He will ask us, "Did you love Me? Were you willing to fight your battles of faith against sin to the very end? Did you trust Me and believe that My resurrection would bring victory in your life? Did you believe that I am Victor?" If we have done so, we shall be like unto Him and see Him as He is in His glory.

When the illiterate patients of the monastery entered the church, they were not to feel even more inferior in the face of the large wood-carving of Anthony. Rather, looking at the risen Lord, they were to be triumphant, in spite of their physical illness and misery. Standing beneath His pierced hands, now raised in blessing, they were to know, "It is not our sickness, our disfigured bodies that are the final outcome, but rather Jesus and His resurrection."

PLATE 25

ANTHONY

When both pairs of wings of the Isenheim Altar were closed, the picture of the crucifixion was in the centre and on either side there was a narrow picture: one of St. Anthony and one of St. Sebastian. Previously the picture of Anthony was on the left and Sebastian on the right, as they are shown here. Today's altar, however, shows the side pictures the other way around (see plate 16).

Gruenewald uses these pictures too in order to express the message of his work of art. Anthony gives the impression of strength and might as he stands here with the abbot's crook in his hand. Gruenewald admonishes us not to domineer, not to seek personal glory or prestige — but rather to humble ourselves, to admit our sins! For what would happen otherwise? In the window behind Anthony we see the devil snorting and smashing the window panes. A poignant reminder that we are in the devil's hand if our pride remains unbroken.

PLATE 26

SEBASTIAN

Sebastian, on the contrary, lets himself be pierced by arrows. He is "crucified with Christ", poor and stripped of all that he had. He entered martyrdom for Jesus' sake, but behind him the heavens are opened and two angels are bringing him a diadem with a large jewel resembling a crown. Because Sebastian kept faith and was loyal to the Lord in the midst of suffering, he received the crown of life (Revelation 2:10 b). When we die with Christ, when we die to self out of love for Him, we shall taste paradise, the kingdom of heaven, and receive the crown of eternal life. The way leading from death to life is open for us, because the Lamb of God went this way for us.

PLATE 27

Worthy is the Lamb
who was slain,
to receive power and
wealth and wisdom and might
and honour and glory
and blessing!

Rev. 5:12

PLATE 28

Other books you may wish to read . . .

by M. Martyria Madauss
THE SHIELD OF FAITH   36 pp. handwritten
For the daily battle of faith against sin.
A sample text: "Be of good cheer, for it is not what you are or do that counts, but what the eternal and merciful God does in you."

by M. Basilea Schlink
BEHOLD HIS LOVE   144 pp.
Nothing can bring us closer to Jesus than meditating upon His Passion, for in doing so we search the depths of His heart. This book will help us to find a warm, vital relationship with our Saviour when we behold His amazing love, which compelled Him to choose suffering and death for our sakes.

IN OUR MIDST —
JESUS LOVES AND SUFFERS TODAY   32 pp.
Jesus still lives and suffers today. The cross is not just a past event of history; we cause Him fresh pain every time we neglect God's Commandments; we grieve Him when we refuse to repent. We fail to recognize Jesus in our midst, because we do not love Him. The message of this booklet is a plea that we should turn to Him for forgiveness and so enter into the personal relationship of love with Him for which we were created.

LET ME STAND AT YOUR SIDE   160 pp.
The Passion narrative, as it is related in this book, movingly takes us into the events of Maundy Thursday and Good Friday as if we were there, and Jesus' sufferings become a challenge for our present-day lives. After reading this book, we can better understand the words, "In comprehending Jesus' sufferings, we learn to love Him more than ever."

MY ALL FOR HIM   160 pp.
"As I read this book, my heart yearned to love our Lord more. But it yearned most hopefully! For Mother Basilea does not merely express the depth of her own love for Jesus. She also shows how we too may ourselves experience it deeply."

PATMOS — WHEN THE HEAVENS OPENED   128 pp.
Vividly and arrestingly Basilea Schlink takes us into the events
of the mighty revelation once given on the island of Patmos.
Today they are beginning to be fulfilled before our very eyes.
This timely book helps us to see the age we are living in and
will be a source of encouragement to us in these dark days. It
gives our generation a completely new perspective to the future
and creates in us a tremendous hope.

THE EVE OF PERSECUTION   90 pp.
Tomorrow we shall be faced with two alternatives: either we
deny and forsake Jesus or we love Him so wholeheartedly that
we are prepared to suffer for Him. Whoever yearns to love
Jesus so much that he will always remain faithful will find the
spiritual help he needs in this book.

THE HOLY LAND TODAY   368 pp.
Revised edition 1975
The Holy Land comes to life — a guidebook with a difference!
Through the prayers and devotional passages the reader is confronted with the challenge of the holy places and the memor-
able events associated with the life and sufferings of the Lord
Jesus. A treasure indeed! Pilgrims will find it an indispensable
companion as they follow in the footsteps of Jesus. Others,
unable to make a pilgrimage, will turn to this book again and
again as they too, in spirit, relive those scenes of long ago. A
book for all who seek a deeper and more personal relationship
to Jesus.   A reader, Jerusalem.

YOU WILL NEVER BE THE SAME   192 pp.
Prescriptions of "spiritual medicine" for 45 different sins. This
intriguing book not only brings to light the sins which mar the
Christian's life, but it also helps us to recognize them in our
personal lives and points out the remedy.